NORTH AMERICAN ANIMALS

Ruby-throated Hummingbirds

by Chris Bowman

BLASTOFF!
3
READERS

BELLWETHER MEDIA • MINNEAPOLIS, MN

Note to Librarians, Teachers, and Parents:

Blastoff! Readers are carefully developed by literacy experts and combine standards-based content with developmentally appropriate text.

Level 1 provides the most support through repetition of high-frequency words, light text, predictable sentence patterns, and strong visual support.

Level 2 offers early readers a bit more challenge through varied simple sentences, increased text load, and less repetition of high-frequency words.

Level 3 advances early-fluent readers toward fluency through increased text and concept load, less reliance on visuals, longer sentences, and more literary language.

Level 4 builds reading stamina by providing more text per page, increased use of punctuation, greater variation in sentence patterns, and increasingly challenging vocabulary.

Level 5 encourages children to move from "learning to read" to "reading to learn" by providing even more text, varied writing styles, and less familiar topics.

Whichever book is right for your reader, Blastoff! Readers are the perfect books to build confidence and encourage a love of reading that will last a lifetime!

This edition first published in 2016 by Bellwether Media, Inc.

No part of this publication may be reproduced in whole or in part without written permission of the publisher. For information regarding permission, write to Bellwether Media, Inc., Attention: Permissions Department, 5357 Penn Avenue South, Minneapolis, MN 55419.

Library of Congress Cataloging-in-Publication Data

Bowman, Chris, 1990- author.
  Ruby-throated Hummingbirds / by Chris Bowman.
     pages cm. – (Blastoff! readers. North American Animals)
  Summary: "Simple text and full-color photography introduce beginning readers to ruby-throated hummingbirds. Developed by literacy experts for students in kindergarten through third grade"– Provided by publisher.
  Audience: Ages 5-8.
  Audience: K to grade 3.
  Includes bibliographical references and index.
  ISBN 978-1-62617-337-8 (hardcover : alk. paper)
  1. Ruby-throated hummingbird–Juvenile literature. 2. Hummingbirds–Juvenile literature. I. Title. II. Series: Blastoff! readers. 3, North American animals.
  QL696.A558B69 2016
  598.7'64–dc23
                              2015028692

Printed in the United States of America, North Mankato, MN.

Table of Contents

What Are Ruby-throated Hummingbirds?

Ruby-throated hummingbirds live in southern Canada and the eastern United States. They fly south to **Central America**.

N
W   E
S

Extinct

Extinct in the Wild

Critically Endangered

Endangered

Vulnerable

Near Threatened

Least Concern

ruby-throated
hummingbird range = ▢

conservation status: least concern

These small birds stay near flowers.
They are found in forests, grasslands,
gardens, and backyards.

Identify a Ruby-throated Hummingbird

green body short wings long bill

Ruby-throated hummingbirds have green heads and backs. Grayish feathers cover their bellies. They have long bills and short legs.

Males have ruby-red **gorgets**.
They have dark **forked tails**.
Females have round tails with
white tips.

gorget

Females grow a little bigger than males. They weigh up to 0.2 ounces (6 grams).

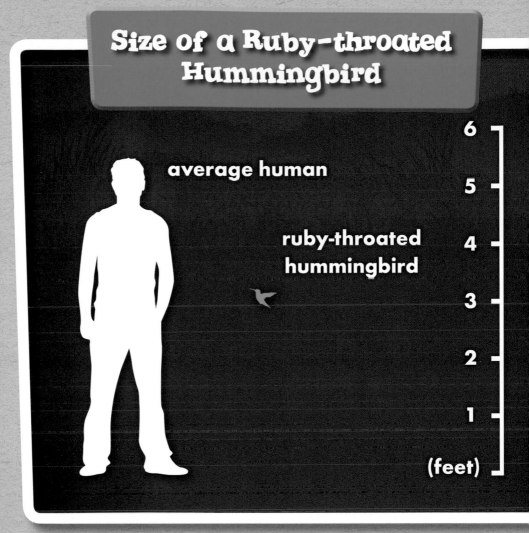

Size of a Ruby-throated Hummingbird

average human

ruby-throated hummingbird

6
5
4
3
2
1
(feet)

Ruby-throated hummingbirds are about 2.8 to 3.5 inches (7 to 9 centimeters) long. Their wings are about 3.1 to 4.3 inches (8 to 11 centimeters) wide.

Red and orange flowers **attract**
ruby-throated hummingbirds.
The birds **hover** to feed on the
nectar of the flowers.

honeysuckle

firepink

trumpet creeper

red morning glory

gnats

bees

These **omnivores** also eat
insects and spiders. They catch
them in the air or pull them
from webs.

Skilled Fliers

Ruby-throated hummingbirds are skilled fliers. They can move in any direction or hover in place. They can even fly upside down.

These birds go from top speed to a full stop in a flash. Their wings beat more than 50 times per second!

In the fall, ruby-throated hummingbirds **migrate** south. Some may fly as many as 1,000 miles (1,600 kilometers) without stopping!

They often double their body size before leaving. This gives them energy for the trip.

After the winter, ruby-throated hummingbirds fly north. Males set up **territories** when they arrive.

Then they put on **courtship displays** for females. They do a series of fast U-shaped dives.

Nests, Eggs, and Chicks

Females build small nests for babies. Then they lay up to three eggs. Soon the chicks **hatch**.

Baby Facts

Name for babies:	chicks
Number of eggs laid:	1 to 3 eggs
Time spent inside egg:	12 to 14 days
Time spent with mom:	22 to 25 days

Females care for their **nestlings** for about three weeks.

Then the **fledglings** take their first flight. They will soon fly south on their own!

Glossary

attract—to draw attention and interest

Central America—the narrow, southern part of North America

courtship displays—behaviors that animals perform when choosing mates

fledglings—young birds that have feathers for flight

forked tails—tails that are split into two parts

gorgets—patches of color on the throats of hummingbirds

hatch—to break out of an egg

hover—to stay in one place in the air

migrate—to travel from one place to another, often with the seasons

nectar—a sweet liquid made by plants

nestlings—chicks that cannot fly yet

omnivores—animals that eat both plants and animals

territories—areas that male ruby-throated hummingbirds defend

To Learn More

AT THE LIBRARY
Alderfer, Jonathan K. *National Geographic Kids Bird Guide of North America: The Best Birding Book for Kids from National Geographic's Bird Experts.* Washington, D.C.: National Geographic, 2013.

Riggs, Kate. *Hummingbirds.* Mankato, Minn.: Creative Education, 2014.

Sill, Cathryn P. *About Hummingbirds: A Guide for Children.* Atlanta, Ga.: Peachtree, 2011.

ON THE WEB
Learning more about ruby-throated hummingbirds is as easy as 1, 2, 3.

1. Go to www.factsurfer.com.

2. Enter "ruby-throated hummingbirds" into the search box.

3. Click the "Surf" button and you will see a list of related web sites.

With factsurfer.com, finding more information is just a click away.

Index